Crows Do Not Have Retirement

CROWS DO NOT HAVE
RETIREMENT

poems

by

David Zieroth

HARBOUR PUBLISHING

Harbour Publishing
P.O. Box 219
Madeira Park, BC
V0N 2H0

THE CANADA COUNCIL | LE CONSEIL DES ARTS
FOR THE ARTS | DU CANADA
SINCE 1957 | DEPUIS 1957

Printed and bound in Canada

Harbour Publishing acknowledges the financial support of the Government of Canada through the Book Publishing Industry Development Program (BPIDP) and the Canada Council for the Arts, and the Province of British Columbia through the British Columbia Arts Council, for its publishing activities.

Cover painting by Marjalena Zieroth
Author photograph by Margery Patrick

National Library of Canada Cataloguing in Publication Data

Zieroth, Dale.
  Crows do not have retirement

  Poems.
  ISBN 1-55017-250-6

  I. Title.
PS8599.I47C76 2001   C811'.54   C2001-910385-9
PR9199.3.Z53C76 2001

To the memory of Maurice Hodgson (1934–1998)

ACKNOWLEDGMENTS

My thanks to the editors of the following magazines and anthologies who published poems (sometimes in earlier versions) from this collection:

Canadian Forum
Canadian Literature
The Dalhousie Review
Event
The Gaspereau Review
Grain
The Malahat Review
Play
Pottersfield Portfolio
Queen's Quarterly
A Matter of Spirit: Recovery of the Sacred in Contemporary Canadian Poetry. Ed. Susan McCaslin. Victoria, BC: Ekstasis Editions, 1998: "The Gulf of Heaven," "Question," "The Poplars of St. Vital," "Three Trees"

The Bedford Introduction to Literature, Fifth Edition. Ed. Michael Meyer. Boston, MA: Bedford Books, 1998: "Time Over Earth"

The Tangled Bed. Victoria, BC: Reference West, 2000: "My First Job," "Crows Do Not Have Retirement," "The Drama"

Thanks as well to the Poetry Evening Group and my friends at Douglas College, with special thanks for the support and editing of Robert Adams, Holley Rubinsky and Russell Thornton. Thanks also to Tom Wayman for his wise counsel.

"Birds appear in poems to show states of mind that go beyond the human."

—Leonard Nathan,
Diary of a Left-handed Birdwatcher

Contents

MY FIRST JOB

The job descends on me
from my father cutting the grass
with his scythe, through my mother
bent over the peas and tossing
weeds where cows take a tongueful
or leave them for the heat
passing over my brothers
home late at night with dollars
in their pockets and up early
to lean into sweat, the job
of killing the kittens
comes down to me

I lure the mother cat away
with fresh cream
and then lift the young up
before their eyes are open
and they look through smoky lenses
and make me fail
the farm overrun, never enough mice
to keep them healthy

and ours not a home
to feed cats more than

milk shot at their wet and open
mouths straight from the cow
or a splash
spilled in an old dish
they lick clean
before going out back
to leap at swallows
dive-bombing their furious tails

I panic at the last
when I stuff them in the sack
and feel their five
bodies tiny as organs twitching
against the burlap—I have already
dug my hole, twisting down
the post-hole digger two feet
then three, and I remember
my mother has drowned one batch
and thinking I can repeat

such a feat, I throw them
into their hole and dump in a pail
of water, but see instead how fast
it flows through the sack
and sand and is gone
the bundles wet, more visible

in their plungings
until I throw on the dirt
again and again and then whack

the ground with the back
of the shovel, and leave that place
and leave the tools for later
to be picked up later, after
I return to the barn to see
the one I left for the mother
looking at the mother's wild eyes
when I approach, seeing
the one I spared, marvelling
at the choice I made

the ground I made holy
and will avoid
for days, weeks, noting never
to dig in that spot, thinking
as I call the dog for our
walk out of the yard and away
to the field, of the tasks
my mother and father carried out
in their obligations year
after year, how much they could do
and not change

Ghosts

THREE TREES

The three trees outside my window
have different views of what I do
but each morning they dote
on the sun, their nearly
identical apical meristems
straining to the light;
afternoons they bend more
toward one another as if
commenting on the deciduous mass
that clutters the ravine,
on sad signs of decay
now the bark beetle has brought brown
to stay. Then
the wind picks up and the three
take to humming, setting off a sound
as old as ice
and without the drumming trouble
of the far-off cottonwoods.
By night they change
and look my way—I swear—
to see what's been denied
to seedlings
intended only to grow just so,
given to one plot,

starting and stopping in this spot.
The large one watches
and comes to know by night
the movements of my to and fro;
I stand sometimes and look beyond
her bulk, hurry on to eat
and shake and bend—and then
grow still
when the green wind comes in
the dark window. I end up always
in bed where the other two
with a tilt of my head
come into view, and all night they
watch over me, in kinship with
my rootedness in sheets,
my only movements slight
or not at all: the flinging out of arms
and dreams of arms
no different from the sway
when birds alight,
big ones to scan
for food, the smaller hearts
gripping hard as they sing.

GHOSTS

Their sudden appearance in me
hasn't stopped; it's just
I'm not moved by their urgent
requests
to give more blood
so they can live that little bit
longer. Still
part of me drops out
of its skin
to make room, and for a time
we share thoughts
that I identify and then discard
until I'm walking alone again.
It's dusk, usually,
and I'm on the prowl
up the back lanes under the influence
of the evening star
beaming down its big light.
Before Father was born
and the ancestors of Mother
slept villages away,
the star shone
and marked the moment
love comes into the world

from day to day.
For others it was merely a rock
that burned,
its bluish flame streaming out
the night a child was born
or one of the old men
stumbled off the winter road.

LETTING MYSELF GO

During the dark rains, for a week
and then a week more
I am mechanical
but health has a threshold
I cannot cross. What is
lacking in me? It is myself
I am missing still. I recall
the day on a street nearby
I was returning videos
and I caught on the air
the scent of a lover I once had
though she did not see me.
Later, I leaned on my fridge
and began to learn its long
lovely note I'm now
too familiar with
and I remembered
wanting to fall on my knees
in the slush because
perfume could fell me so, a man
quivering in the muck
of an afternoon street, wrappers
drifting past him,
shoppers turning to see

at last a spectacle to carry home
and discuss with partners,
what it could mean, that man
letting himself go,
his weakness draining out
to join the gutter water
on its way to the sea
which will take
whatever is given no matter
how many pieces there may
happen to be.

THE POPLARS OF ST. VITAL
for Walter and Tashi

These trees catch at winds
flung out of sky and sun
in gusts aimed to be elsewhere;
they define the street
by bowing to the park.
And I bend, too, and see
my shoes need replacing soon,
which means going to the stores
with the money required
for leather uppers,
which means: where leather
originates—and the factory!
For relief I return to my friend,
who has somehow untangled himself
from the race but without denying
any of us—
which leads to talk.
His dog returns with wetness from the river
and flings it happily about,
and we raise our hands to ward off
the worst of it, not wanting
his little joke;
he is already composing

23

intelligent dog-thoughts
about this trip, the pleasant
weariness that will flop him down,
the old shoe he tossed once and
left, the other dogs he spoke to
in appropriate ways so they would know
his master and his friend
were not to be dallied with,
the sense of the circle he made
once again, how sufficient it felt,
especially the paths through the poplars
many others have taken.
So we follow the happy dog
and I unburden myself without
dumping; we smell the river
and are grateful although
its raw red line
can reek of sewage, more risk
in this long life on a small planet
judged scientifically to be alone
even as our hi-tech runners
scuff along the bank
and our inner chemistry
strains hugely for
some cosmological love
untouched by how we change.

THE WHISTLER

I am reading at my window
some sad tale and these words:
"It will probably take
a thousand years for human beings
to give up
            the last remnants
of the idea that they contain
a spark of the divine"

when whistling so sweet
floats out of the dark
I turn away
from thoughts altogether
to follow the silver ribbon
the man tosses
on the night, pouring out
what others say
is never there

and if I agree?
Then I've been too long
listening to silence
and I put down my book
and step out to find the source

so sure one glance
at his face
will brighten
a winter's night

or failing contact there
I'll measure what I am
against the rain at least
against the lamps in every house
and no one on the street
and all the stars too far

THE GULF OF HEAVEN

Between what we need to know
and what we come to believe
lies the Gulf of Heaven
we cross daily
swimming to that further shore
which bears its joyful name
because only there are we free
from the uncertainty
after the last bit of love
lets us down for the day
and we call on
the reserves
to arise.

Once I thought
I could push myself across
by myself: I was young,
I had my father's voice
to make me think
I was a big tough lad.
But blood bubbles
into ideas, and not one
helped me swim the expanse
after zoology class,

in the cold, on Furby Street,
imagination and Sheri Denbo
pushing against me
as if they were
answers.
        Now I move from
what I hope is truly true
to what I discover
I believe. And I have begun to believe
in the breast stroke and the butterfly stroke
because of their beautiful names
and because heaven must be
perfectly conjured and framed,
each wave falling back
beside my head to show me
glowing green land
and the hot shore.

QUESTION

1.

Is my soul a cup of milk
that once taken

spreads into every capillary
giving me a personality

to fit Friday
or Monday with all its moods?

2.

When I was afraid to say
I had a soul, did I imagine

I would leave it in a cafeteria line
with the half-eaten muffin

for some white-clad worker
to carry off?

When I was young enough to believe
reason, why didn't reason

bear me up the stairs
of my father's house

to sleep the sleep of peace,
happy logic in my head?

3.

When this soul came to me
what animal peace

fell from me, and when I fell in love
how did my soul know

that here was chemistry
come round again to try

joining another
it could never finally touch?

4.

Can't electrons alone
animate my hand

so it can place and put,
stroke or strike?

A man comes to a woman
and the cells divide—could you fix

a more peculiar plan?
Or imagine

the entry of the soul
at some disputable moment

and without fanfare
in bedrooms, guest

houses everywhere? The non-thing
among hips and moans?

5.

What if I slip one night
into a dream and bang my head

so hard I leave my body behind?
Is my soul this dream of light

returning to itself?
Is it time

carried in a pocket
and going farther away?

6.

When my soul leaves me
will it fly like an owl

to the nearest height of land
to watch,

its golden eyes
solemn but without grief?

Body floating,
apparently set to drift,

I look into your eyes,
—and why can't I see you

before you came here
by saying

mother, father,
birthmark, skin?

7.

My own soul,
did it grow out of childhood

or was it bestowed?
Has it always been?

My old dog when I was young,
did he know?

Did my mother?
Did everyone

have some part lighter
than bone, longer than blood?

SOUNDS LIKE

. . . a car coming close and
passing away, its wet tires
a long descending hiss

. . . a single-engine prop plane
straining to rise above
the bridge, its cargo

a pilot and passenger
whose hearts beat hard
against what falls away

. . . wind in the conifers
saying its prayers:
now, now, and then, and then

again to the rain-laden needles
and the rebounding boughs
and the hidden finches

. . . clouds amassing and
intermeshing, soft boulders
releasing and rebuilding

. . . a crow announcing
presence is enough
while we wait

Ravine: I

METHOD

> "He never could tell when his heart might drop again
> and leave him unable to remember any need to do
> anything."
>
> —*A. L. Kennedy,* "True"

I come to the steps of the old house
in the park looking for
an exact anger
that once found and felt
will lead me to the next
exact anger and the next.
But here the sun's afternoon angle
promises more than heat,
its language
warmly metaphoric,
its trees casting long
layers of light
on the lawn
and the beginning evening breeze
brings a child's taunt:
"Paul is a baby! Paul is a baby!"
and a father's voice
raised: "Yes, it will stay;
now leave it." Reasons for living
I'll deal with later

after this moment
turns its thought toward
the question of overcoming
attachment, but listen,
here is where some of you
should disembark, having tasted
sweat along my lids
which a hot afternoon has placed there
not from my walking and working up
those fit feelings of physical righteousness
but from the shakier inside
working its way out and staining a reader's
forward view with a colour not too nice—
so off with you, then!—and no blame,
but if you stay with me now,
you've given up the right
to speak against
the soft-sentence version
of what is felt: the will
to energy
dead, the natural
turn of the mind
caught in a cant
out of fashion but right at home
as if I'd been reared by folks different
from these home-going, lawn-crossing ones,
their bats and balls and towels

announcing father's less cross if he knows
light this time of day
illumines with Disney
clarity but gives as well the gift of air
to create dimension; no, I've been raised
on the Prussian principle of bold stinginess,
wind from the plains
cold when I for one
wish to lie close
not to another but to the ground
where I can name the flies
that buzz me. But first
a tour! Of my neighbourhood,
so you, determined reader,
can see where I walk
these streets,
perhaps to spy your house
or an old couple passing by;
a baby's arms, open to summer,
branching from its sides: pink
cactus; then a fat blond child
wet from the sprinkler,
thin polyester pj's
clinging to her skin: she's digging
some sliver in her bulging hand
fully focused until she swerves
her gaze onto me; the biker

clattering up the street and rolling
his machine across the sidewalk
to be welcomed home
by the hollyhocks
tall as the shapeless house they hide,
the gas tank of his bike
dressed in purple tear drops
like dashes of blood
slanting back in the wind
from hands held high
to grip the reins;
the oldest man on the block still pushes
his mower up the slope of his walk and
when he looks up
he's grimace and teeth:
what an old, hard-working smile
looks like; the guy
in green shorts, pink top
stretches tight its little
alligator—not afraid to bend down
and stick his bum in the street
as he picks at the weeds
near his toes; Jenn Scott's
name on a yellow symbol
of a fish at the entrance
to a street-drain to warn us
we must not pour down death,

must not play God.
So if it's anger we come to
on this trek, it's not the flash
that burns out the sky and consumes
the undeniable end of things
in the plunge toward what's coming our way
but can't be seen on the usual size screen
most of us are watching;
more like the slow drip
of generation into generation
that helps me clean
the bathroom, and the rest of the apartment
can wait. A billionaire from Hong Kong
has bought the building but I can move,
I'm on the top floor
and I can fly. I've phoned one daughter
to say I loved her
and she said in return
she loved me—and the exchange
was easeful and true;
the younger one I've helped
out of a jam: neighbour's gone away
and she volunteered to take on
their cat—feeding, petting: prevention
to keep it from going wild,
rumoured to be its response
to prolonged abandonment;

smart move, I'd say. So
I'm full of daily events, some
secretly life-giving, drawing sweetness
out of me, as my spider-grass
kinks its leaf one day
and sends out a bud
to meet the potential
bane that can come
to new blooms. Imagine my children
coming upon me flat on the floor,
red in the tub:
what they would carry
the moment a word went in
and hatched, stayed with them
through the first
anniversary, the second, the memory
transfiguring itself, a living stalk
sending out its own runners to creep
and trap and hold back
natural joy until it was gone.
You picture this, patient reader,
no doubt imagine this lot
on yourself at least once,
not among those
who never give in to a thought
that curves and takes on

a life of its own and thus demands
a death of its own.
You and I took extra shots in the womb
of Daddy's zest,
Mummy's heart beating
always here, here, here
and when we bother with beyond
for a moment alone
before sun-up or at night
—not for long—what we hear
is soon enough gone, drowned
by blood rushing eardrums
and the simple surprise of
what the eye can find
even in the dark: the clock beams
on the bookcase, the curtains
reveal a night breeze; trees
strong as grandfathers
draw us back into sleep,
and our dreams
are not clutter out of which
comes the next day's crush.
And walking through the neighbourhood
—still with me?—I look for
one stark thought I can clash against
but recall instead how

something leaked into me
from the gene pool, tightened
each day a little more
until I was shrink-wrapped
and laughable, the skin around my face
pulled down, my exoskeleton self
not too good either. I worried
I was missing what all other men
seemed to have: themselves
and a way of walking
through the mall that said:
Milady, I have the most amazing balls
loaded for your pleasure and your kin
and I can compose your two-note song
on the linen so sweetly
that you give me
a moment I go blank
and in rushes love, out bolts
the mud-blood—
and the books from smiling people
tell how to cope.
I'm reading in the mall;
I glance up
to the mirror above the best-sellers, to see
my unbelieveable look: grumpy,
cagey, selfy, silly,

woody, wobbly and dick.
I close the book and return to
checking faces as they go by: that mouth
plunges, this mouth (all straight
across but pulling up) stays in place
wanting a bargain that will
give hope to hope—and where
does he bury his rage? In his cat,
his car, his sport, his wife,
his secret hand, food,
his lawn? Which we are passing now,
green gem that signals to the universe
its code of order, boxer shorts,
tools arranged on the downstairs wall,
and a dream far off, speeding out to Mars.
It's like that for all of us
some time: we stop believing
our own stories and get
wild that our selves
didn't work, that not enough people
felt good to us long enough,
that it was just us
everywhere in our consciousness
and that everyone else was just them;
and in the moment of surrender
after waking when I am without words

and only images
flock around, without my story,
I am naked, inconsolable, under attack,
self-indulgent—yet most myself?
I wake and before the words begin
three doors marked
pain, pain, pain
wait to be opened.
In what night was I deemed
its carrier? Was there a congregation
of beings, lights, flashes,
that touched my father's shoulder
and turned to my mother
for entry? How much can I lay
at their bedside,
those big humans
—yet sometimes what I see
is love: their goof-waltzing
in the kitchen, better than their
smooth displaying
dance in town;
and sometimes what I see is dark and grim
as they took bad weather
on the chin and fell in
on themselves—
we all get a knock on the head.

I look at my father's
burning, the more constant less
spectacular show of my mother's flame,
what they had to work with
and what they worked against
and how they were in their lives
and how mine was not
headquarters,
how irreparable
my one-ness got to be
as I grew up and they did not
—and while I often think now
of laughter, card games
at a good volume of life,
what comes through
is a grieving
that the wholeness of promise
could not blitz fears;
and the arc of their lives
is the arc of every life
including mine, and the variations
don't count
before the pattern
we rail against,
stepping on and off the story-line
and by fancy-dancing

hope to feel truly
what is
and what is dying.
Reasons for living
come later, as does perspective
and humour, and even the arts
of steeling oneself nicely,
but not now, not right now
in your head: you
fall away, nothing's holding up,
others have nets by now,
their groups, smiles
and ways of taking an eyeful of death
and still winging on.
Yes, love makes light,
love meets the day.
Love can hold you
in the night like a good song says.
Love can find you or not.
I'll okay this version anyway,
okay these irritations,
poisons, pleasures
—needs, one to walk
and walk, discover I am
not the successful community member
but what the neighbourhood needs:

him who passes a drift-bit of talk
and constructs a life, the smells
of kitchens, the calls of kids;
and out on the field
at Fen Burdett Stadium the young men
love to play baseball in the rain,
it makes them stronger, more real,
beer better at the end,
and if questions arise,
at least tired muscles soon
pull the brain into sleep.
I'm telling you
things you don't want to know
about another person, I'm saying
in this age we all want
one finger in some wound
and will travel the world
to find the right one. I know
the age of confession has passed,
is passé, but my friends
can't bear to listen
and so, reader, you are my confessor,
only you can hear me out
and I reach for you across the page
and pull you in, let me do it,
I've got an ache

you can make better
just by taking me in—and you know
we're all feeling snarled though
many of us are tough
for the sake of
others around us. Run your tongue
over the morbid
and the mean, the little hole
at the edge of the hairline
out of which you fly.
But where does "I" go
if anywhere and who to believe if anyone
and why not wait to find out later?
And so, as they say,
most of my healing is done
at night, and it is these exaggerations
I rise up from Woolco sheets to embrace,
preferably with a flourish
that gives meaning
or at least the strength of meaning
further on in the day. Yes,
I can feel it now
yearning in me
as I look high up into the face of the
Molecule—could be, you know
since one by one they are replaced,

the electrons that sing in me
their little steady hymn
get trucked away
into the blood, and new ones
arise unmanufactured
to walk the same race.
Do you recall walking this way—
with such thoughts in your head?
And I'm by your side
gently pointing out the way it looks:
a nightmare here
and over there a sinking of the heart
we were not prepared for,
a lump of coal growing
in your lover's breast,
a June
wet and ungiving
waiting to be cleaned off
my files, drawing my attention
to please note
I'm still flying
on the propulsion
of my last life crisis: so zoom
I live, and live.

FRAGMENTS OF FALL

"evenings go down the steps and the steps are live flesh"
—*Czeslaw Milosz*, "The Song"

On Michaelmas I walk down 15th Street,
not in its centre, not even
on the sidewalk
but on the grass or what passes for grass
between sidewalk and street.
I take the back lanes
where birds still congregate
and gabble. I open my jacket
like Superman
and my heart's dragon leaps out
—for this is his season
to get purchase
in a neighbour's back yard,
among the compost and the weedy
greenhouse, the trashy margins,
red berries of the mountain ash
on asphalt, black squirrels
running pell-mell on the walls.

He vaults out,
twitching at the perfume

of rotting fruit. Two kids on bikes
come up the lane and neither
notices how rare the light
has been rendered, nor do they halt
his tail thrashing like a cat's
or the apples going down whole
and untasted.

At the entrance to the ravine
the sharp stones gather
to light the way down
and notify my feet
of the slope between grey and green;
a curve of dirt
under a soft overhang
calls me to itself
in the nerves,
and some word I heard
dreams on and on; a sentence
I can only diagram
in the dark
gets obsessed again
to step into the next story:
how the grass

made the sun blaze,
and children spent lifetimes
reaching us from there.

Then I wake up
and have become a rock.
I have no power on my own
to move. Not much happens
in this warm bed
but neither can I extend a hand to hit
the snooze: the news goes on
and the music can't soothe
or awaken. Eventually I
melt, not down, but out
until I'm suddenly at the mirror
and begin to understand
both the commercial of this face
with its taxable morning breath
and the thing come closest
to nothingness all night.

So these lonely years
I thought I needed
some years ago

and which I imagined then
would give me a spell
—it's almost true—
now I turn my head slowly
to match the glide of the eagle
as he passes my window, crows
diving at his royal head
and yet he seems scarcely to notice
the fury of their black
cork-screwing as if the wind tunnel
of his making
turns them to rags
and they are begging him
for a hold in the rear turbulence
of his sure and steady flight
as if he carries
one shining thought
that pulls him along
and which the crows dive for,
knowing just a touch
will give them light enough
to flash their wings
and make silver in the sun,
coin they'll spend
later, bragging among friends.

A day of rainy sun
and birds
still singing, which tells me
they like good weather, too,
whether their mates are interested or not,
so many of them
getting ready to depart,
south or otherwise. No one asks them
how many times today
on a scale of one to ten
they slipped below five.
Tufts of blown cloud
pass overhead, setting up
an unrepeatable pattern.
I walk and yearn and long
without object:
no robin redbreast can hitch me
to wind, a star, or cloud
sailing out of town
to crash over mountains
or make a statement coming down.
It washes past me
taking my humour,
made to babble at last

among the roots of the ravine
where the big rats are charmed
into slowness
by the weird new nearness
of a watery human voice.

I pop open the window, lean out,
take in the mountain
to balance on my optic nerve
and press myself out.
Loss of self enters
last, after dropped keys,
driving back from summer,
longing for a favourite plaid.
And then finding and wearing
and washing and washing
and one day cutting
and ripping into strips,
placed in the closet, fragrant
cedar and cloves.

Any day now
the random universe
spinning past

will drop a block of frozen waste-water
through my roof and kill me
as I'm brushing my teeth,
getting ready to dream
under a blanket of stillness,
leave my window open
all night; the air comes in
in little puffs
from the mountain, fresh
with coming winter,
its trees not green
but shaggy shapeshifters,
a branching finger
poking an open mouth.

Taking my list of things to do
for a walk
so it will slim down
on its own, its endorphins
set me free. Instead
geese above the clouds
fly south without us;
leaves on the poplars
stop to hear, then

turn from the sky
for the first time.
Stop this walking and walking,
self-talking,
and I'll find what's divine in me
down in the ravine
where I touch the tall
cottonwoods and feel them
touch me, shipping down
from the torn clouds
what they can.

To be able to say
"Oh, that was years ago"
and still not yearn for
the shining child,
the boy like a listening post
among adults who shrivelled
or exploded, men first;
the man today in the yellow Pinto
sunken down in the broken seat
leaned back as the wheel
rose up to save him.
I ask my students
"Where's the depth?"
and its opposite,

the lightness of air,
bright leaves
on the pond, and the ducks
no longer frenzied
by water speaking wet.

By now the weather has driven
the fat flies into the warmth
of my rooms, but they are slow
and drugged by the cold
in their fuzzy bones—if bones they had.
They're going into oblivion
from natural causes:
my mighty roll
of the *Sun* or just the eventual
descent into the corner
where they throw themselves down
on their backs and wait
for the broom.

On a small scale it's a grand
performance: first the drone
of low-bomber buzzing,
then crashing into

mirrors, bookshelves, doors,
and always the fatal tone
of their decline,
this dizzy spinning
on the linoleum with a cat
flicking its paw
and turning away to its own
soft chow.

Who among us will become
the man I met on Mahon?
He presented red wrinkles
but his "How are you?"
lifted and sang out fine.
I just know
all his life he saw that face
coming and turned his attention
to the sound he sent out of his world
into yours, whoever you may be,
his wife, his son
who early understood
his own fate
would be wattles
where once his mum

pressed her lips and tossed him
out from bed
into Father's
cardigan arms.

The wall of green
outside my window drops
although this morning's breeze
still ran a fluid shiver
through its mass, an undersea jelly
of light,
light we give back
this time of year,
shoving it under the ground,
carrying it inside
to crinkle and wait
for the accidental brushing-by
of a child.
Rain strokes the bare trunks
all night
and water-marks
on cement buildings
creep down.
Sunday morning

in bed, listening, sounds
good as a woman.

Do this, do that,
do this, do that,
and I do and I do
but I cannot subside
—this sounds like—
—this feels like.
I turn back the clock,
motor through a zone of stink
out of the city,
then return through the industrial donut
around row houses.
It's raw everywhere I look
on that drive: large peaked warehouses
rising on the landfill site.
Wet trucks all around; soon
the evening snow.

DREAMING AND WAKING

"We fall *into* something, falling asleep, not *out* of
things. Dreams are already there, beckoning . . ."
　　　　　　—*John Updike*, "Falling Asleep Up North"

Between dreaming and waking
leaps a spark,
chemistry
between shores,
encoded
but not completely known:

I am out in the city
in my bathrobe, and no lights
guide my way. I carry in my right hand
a loaf of bread among the dark walls
and darker parks,

trying to find the way home.
People on platforms built
for such purposes are lounging
as they wait for first light

and though I am not menaced by them
I am cautious, aware how ill-prepared
I appear in my flapping

blue robe, my bread already
moulding in its bag.

I take steps down
and find at last a railway track.
Many of us are backed up here,
waiting for a train
to come ploughing through.

Eventually I cross with the flood
of others, and I overhear
their stories and most tell of
the death of one man,
and our hearts are pierced.

I split off from that crowd
and feel my way along,
enter the back of a cathedral
and see the congregation
behind a gauzy curtain

and leave by a side door
holding keys, many shiny meanings
that gleam in the sun,
light that makes the ground
around me rich and sweet.

Four chalk mallards
of descending size
decorate and cross my bedroom wall
—and come unhinged at night
and fly out my window
onto nearby waters.
The largest holds his wings high
and back, breast cutting the spray,
feet and tail
flattening water;
beauty is fluid,
even in his follower whose wings
spread to take a chance
on the rising currents
coming from the land
—he loves the speed—
but the third grows smaller and
turns away, as if surprised
by the shot of a hidden gun,
the startled kink of his neck
suggesting death nearby or
closer; while the last,
half the size of the first,
more a teal than a mallard,

flings after the others,
always a lost little one.
I have asked him
to employ his wings
and wake me
from the blue green pond where I am apt
to linger, listening for the lapping
of water in the muskrat run.
It is his upwind fly-past
that brings me back
across my bed, arm crooked
over my eyes.

The coming of the rats—
although much anticipated
and often feared
as an event not to be dealt with
alone—occurs unexpectedly
at the moment of dusk
when the light is dim again
and the eyes, unsure at first
can't acknowledge the movement
at the curb or the shadow
at the base of the living room wall.

The holes they have chewed
in the backs of my closets,
the nests they have made
from the linen, and the smell
of their numbers
circling under my bed
—none of these enters me
like their smiles
for they have come to my pillow
to share their teeth with me
and to drape their tails
in the palm of my hand.
I jerk,
electrons under each knee
firing away.

The gifts walk out from
behind the tree, boxes mainly
in colour
and I have to ask
"Who's the big one for?"
the one upon which the others
stack. I start to shred the pretty
paper. I'm just a kid.

An airplane appears
and it's mine! It does nothing
but suggest; not even lights
flash when I push
the rubber wheels
on my mother's shiny floors.
Then I'm changing
into a bigger me on the outside
but the plane stays in my hand
until one day
it can't be found.
Someone took it when I was gone
and passed it
to a younger me, and this chain
of child to child continues;
its propellers no longer work
except when a tot enters
the exact historic time
it came into being,
resources pouring out of the ground
into little shiny icons
we placed about our homes, our family
one by one touching them before bed.

I have lost the children
entrusted to me; we are crossing
the city, and the moppets,
strung out behind me,
begin to vanish. Some I know
have just dropped down
to play behind the trunks
of the big cedar trees,
and I go back to pick them up
and while I am reaching for their hands
others run up the steps
of nearby houses and knock wildly
on the door—and when the door opens
they are gone. Some charges
just walk away with other men,
and I can't tell from this distance
are they legitimate fathers
or should I shout for help?
I hold articles of clothing
in each hand—a cap, a tiny umbrella,
velcro mittens that stick to me—
and when I look at these
I panic and begin to run.
I shout their names,
but no one in the neighbourhood

comes out of the houses,
only curtains in front windows
fall back to block me out.

I am in charge
of a large trunk
which holds several old
and important books

plus the wedding dress of a colleague;
she is worried I will not manage
the task, and on the following grounds
she makes her case:

I am unusually small,
less than a pet; I can only touch
the knees of those around me,
some of them jeering

as I make my way up stone steps
with the trunk. I feel drugged
by the air surrounding me
which seems yellow

although not harsh, not yet,
when I realize I can lessen the load
by dumping the books;
impossible

to ditch the dress:
I'm held in trust
to someone I hardly know
and about whom I am not allowed to ask.

So I drag a froth of lace and satin
and crinoline, and the books left behind
become a tall brown block
just off the main path.

I am on the bus to Montreal,
not a Greyhound but rather
a Bedford, a new bus line
I thought I'd try, when a man

comes out from the front
to ask me questions about my income
and since I'm a student
he decides I'll have to get off

in Fort William, that I'm simply
not good enough to go all the way
and that I need more money in my life
to ride with Bedford.

It's then I notice the passengers
are wearing suits, and all
are men, each with files and papers
spread about on the plush seats.

I ring the bell, climb down
and begin crashing through brush
at the side of the road. Soon
I come to a farmhouse

and in the kitchen I see
another man
grey and swaying,
wailing from some pain

as if sick or drunk; around him
a fog floats so I can't see clearly;
occasionally a woman
wrings her hands

in a shaft of light.
I watch this man for hours
and then am released
back to the countryside

where I discover
a path among boulders,
two figures walking with me,
slightly behind, to left and right

and neither tells me where to go,
that destination now
so obviously up ahead,
in the direction two dogs

come racing from, leaping past me in adoration
to catch the hand signals
I am sending, then running back
to lick me, their leader whom they love.

Ravine: II

MEN

At a gathering of men who consider
the penis a marvel of liquid
engineering, I wander off
to the kitchen and the women
who talk about the coven and the oven
and what
comes out, the place so gleaming I skid
on the watery floor and love the chat
and want *cosy* and find
other men want this too: where lust
is love and love intertwines
and settles us into
work and food—and children
under illness turning us wild
like a flake of rust in one eye.
And these babies grow or die
in your arms, your wife breaks
and then gets up and rewinds
though not all the way in every year
in huts and houses, floors of
vinyl or dirt. It takes a child
to feel the nearness of ruin
always at the door, a fear
knocking to say he's here,

his hand on the jamb, ready to push
and come right in without pause,
his long white reach for
someone you love, your youngest
not yet ready, mush on her bib
one tiny shoe in oblivion
—or the oldest someone in the car
trapped in a headlight that leads to
a rib smashed in high gear,
others passing on to well-lit
cheerfulness and rest a man imagines
but only if his bit
of time has limited calamity.

CROWS ABOVE

At a gathering of crows above
our heads, the bird lice intermingle
and carry on in these wolves
of the air whose cries
mock our own low murmurings
when salt from my mouth seeks salt
from yours, my hand twisting dirt
to keep myself in me. The crows
come close and want to know
what tidbit they might spot
coming off us, what shiny sweat
might hit a leaf and make it grow
so fast they'd need to pluck it up
and make it prize possession number one
in their stick nest, their gawky young
coming out of eggs and into the sun
that glimmers off their parents'
military black as yet undone
by the shining of that leaf
—and these babies
come to song much sooner than
expected, sooner yet they loot
and tear at things found flat and
dead, coming together into a murder

every now and then. While here below
I discover your very
breath is tinged with the grave,
my toenails dig into your calves,
and the way I slurp my porridge
causes you to pack and leave.
Out the window we throw old love
as if it never was much,
a brainless midge ablaze
in the storm of what we always
are: ourselves we can't lift
into the air to catch the gift
of light above the caws and caws.

PATERFAMILIAS

At a gathering of women
I am suddenly eating spicy food
from their fingers, struck
by their no-fear children
and their love of mocking
calling me prince and king
of the night when I'm in no mood
to go head to head without luck
on my side, I'm not invincible,
but my eye returns to the kids
squirting through the grass.
So much makes me sigh
around women, I generalize
and romanticize, enter
the myth in which I am paterfamilias
and where sons and nephews
clutch the edges of my domain and cry out
for special favours from my purple
realm and then realize I'm all
magnanimous anyway and begin to grouse
about arrangements, join a circle
with their wives and turn me out
so I become a bum, dead pale on the street.
I turn from women to food; a louse

can't live on what I grub
from the backs of greasy eateries,
all the while recalling the sheets
I once rolled within, clean
and sweet and cool, to which
she came to slip around me,
hold me happy and hard, telling
the story we had lived till then
against my ear, the touch there between
my heart and hers starting snuggle
and sweat, her skin and feeling
so giving that upswell
redeems unregard.

PEDESTRIAN

At a gathering of pedestrians
I see we each carry a balloon,
some interesting, some not,
the red light on stop, my thoughts
on hopes and prayers:
to be loved by the woman
who reaches the far sidewalk first
and not to tire out
and not to panic when she shies away,
her day in a glare
of spite and I become an also-ran.
I try to head off her pout.
I spend my Saturday
focused on her onslaught
of needs and errors that burst
my way; all afternoon
she's in her room packing dresses
and perfume and swinging the case
down the stairs and into the cab,
her face streaked and smeary
and leaving me powerless
to fill the space
except with the souvenir of
bafflegab that runs through my mind

—such as now
out on the street, strolling forth
and building up a sense of ease,
false as it is—because I want
to cuddle up and touch her hair
and know she's in the room
nearby, the window designed
to shower light on her arms
so when I stop by the door, idly
passing from bed to book,
head aching from career and gloom
I catch her stance and for
a moment am a grateful, quaking lamb.

Ravine: III

HOW TO BEGIN

I am waiting for my life to begin.
It will begin tomorrow or the day after,
not today although
I arose in hopes and my dreams
clung to me and held me to the bed
for a moment, but by first tea
I was exactly where I had been
the day before, not yet real
not begun or able to begin
and by lunch when I unrolled
my waxed-paper meal and set it
on the desk covered with paper
and clips and pens and pencils
and flat white screens in the corner
I had still not begun, although I could feel
a little panic growing, that much
was beginning to grow, alive
in a way that I was not, saying
its name in me, although had you come
to the door and looked in I would have smiled
and even stood up and made a space
shaken your hand, offered
some share of my meal, our wit and talk
helping us both before you went back

to your place and I to mine
and found it was always just me
in here, in this room of my thinking
with no one to take a little
of the weight, no lover or worker
in here, just the chairs and the pins
and the posters and the papers
and the sun coming in always
more of a mockery as if to say
I was locked away—until the phone rang
and called me out of such a thought
and I shared myself around with a voice
that said the happy things, hung up
myself and went relieved back to desk
and chair and again felt my body slow
until it stopped at the crossroads
that went first to panic and then
out the door and down the hall
to the person in charge to ask her
when can I begin, when can I begin
and she reassured me I have started
and am doing a fine job, a most
thorough job, and she lists my many
triumphs, some going back to the very day
I began in this room, and she tells me
I should go home now, take the final hour

and catch the sun, stop on the way
at some playful spot by water or near
children, get out a bit, don't think.

WHAT TO DO

I am trying to get it all done.
Not just the nails and hair and teeth
of my body that demands
me in the morning
and then in the night as if it were
two different bodies, each wanting
a life of its own rid of
the counterpart that drags
away from the pure clean
drive of the moment—
and where the body lives
clothes need laying out
and cleaning, dust gathers
and can't be gotten rid of for good
it's so persistent
the way other entities are not:
money   health love
while the dust reminds me
time is being used up
falling on the geraniums
and on the photographs
on my face as I sleep and sometimes
dream of a place where
deeds once done

stay permanently held
and formed and without
their little voices to cry out
for my attention when I waltz past
on my way to one further task
already risen to the topmost
of the list, at least on the list
that gets scratched down, not
the list I avoid
except when my upper head
opens wide and out rushes
the urge that insists
I climb onto memory and
tamp down and rearrange
until it's just a part of things
—and I get beyond such thinking
with the little business of going
down the stairs and into the air
to notice how the car shines
how fast it can take me
down the road, the sweet feelings
of leaving behind
the dust with its claim
so unlike my shoes and scarves
my gloves in the hall
the anorak awaiting weather

all so clear they never allow me
to confuse sun with hail
or a drift of blossoms with snow.

WHEN TO STOP

Why not stop just for a moment?
All this personal mumbo-jumbo
about what I should or should not
be doing, where I should be
going or even if this is
a journey at all, and then
what this moment is meant
or not meant for, where the light
on the back of my hand comes from
if it's something bigger than me
or just something other
or whether we can know
what we know if we haven't already
known ourselves or worse—
why not just take a break
from thinking over and over
and not getting down to the
first sticky spot of thought
that binds us right to the ground
we find ourselves thinking of—
just grant a little slip
into silence on the inside
not just the silence of not saying
much but the real relief of

no more warblings in the brain
but of course we all know too much
and know as well we can't
stop just a little except in sleep
can't stop for a moment until/
unless we take the biggest stop
of all, the point where we
get off the conveyance entirely
and step down onto the unknown
—and then what if we find ourselves
weeping wildly even there, cut off
and apart and without link
not just to another or any other
but to ourselves who seem to have
gone on without us, our
bones still sitting up
and bouncing along, the same old
driver up ahead not bothering anymore
to call out the stops because
all the stops are now the same,
the same, the same, and we're
just little tiny men and women
after all, we're nothing more
except once or twice maybe when
we turn to one another and let
shine out through our eyes what

we feel, and some shine joy
and some shine horror and either way
we are the driven and unstoppable.

WHERE TO GO

Might as well go somewhere.
Strap the rockets onto my heels
and take to the sky, roaring over
the city and the water
and still going: nothing here
and nothing there so might as well
be there, landing now
in an old medieval town,
flowers in pots, and dogs
trotting by masters on the street
noses on the ground and catching
whiffs of fish and fur
and the sun hot on both
on all of us, my sleeves rolled up
and in the way ahead
the biggest hole in the ground
I've ever seen, one a German
bomb might have made
landing a day ago
when I was still cooped up
in my hut across the sea—
and I go scrambling over rubble
into the depths of this otherwise
proud old town, and when I'm

in the black hollow of itself
I can't hear the traffic
can't hear the sea or birds
either, no wind carries
into this heavy air and the smell
that comes up burns my eyes
tastes of iron on my tongue
though welcome on my lips
as if I need in my diet
some extra shot of good grounding
soil, the kind made for me
to lie on and listen to with my ear
against the stones
that break through the mauve
darkness here and there
giving a glow because they are not
black but rather rubbed smooth
and full of hardness which I try
to get into myself right then
placing my head on the biggest
block and pulling at it
and willing it to give a little
and enter some speck or molecule
into me, along the rim of the brain
watch it spin for a moment
then drop down through the veins

into the flesh and finally into
the mouth where I hold it like a pit
on my way up to the light.

WHY WAIT?

Because the mood changes.
An angel lifts her dark hand
off my shoulder, and with her other
pokes me in the backside
says get out there, engage
and what happens then is
summer surrounds me, fecundity
leans on its elbow and
without moving a finger
ducklings appear on the pond,
where once gravel ruled
now is soft grass,
in trees the crows congregate
and come winging by to scold,
the foxgloves reach up
and pluck down blue and spread it
across their petals soft as cheeks
—and having seen that, yeah,
the world remains close and dear
I check one tentative time
on my thinking, on the words
that are surely mine, although
when I am not kind sometimes
I cannot call them mine

silly me silly bugger
talking in there
willing to take up
residence amid the various poses
and poems, words that clunk
down in little chunks
and won't move except to grow
more sticky on the page
so of course
while the view is sometimes
very clear, a winter clarity
across which snow falls
in its crystalline
unwavering down
into the open mouth of a child
with tongue poised
to catch the angles and the many
forms, each one entering
into him and suggesting
later in his life when he's
waiting for some wonderment
that here's a possible way,
try this way—so while this cold
is sometimes the view I am
I also see the slush season
and the grey words

—but not today which is long
with sun who sends out songs
for birds to sing near me.

Prayers

ORACLE IN THE MALL

I am waiting at the bookstore
when a pursed-mouth former
neighbour approaches, peers:
"You've aged"—as if I cared right then,
as if the real point
weren't her effrontery.
A haircut snips away
that spiky grey but she stays with me
when I ask the mirror where:
in my hair? in my skin? yes, yes.
My eyes? She looked
at my left earlobe—had it aged too?

Did I ask her to interfere?
I did not look up
to bring her attention
down upon my head. I don't want
her story at all. Was she carrying
When Bad Things Happen to Good People?
She assumed a direct line to the divine
worthy of my fear. I won't listen
when she tells me what I never want to hear.
I want the voice to reach me
from the sky: *Hold on, son.*

Later in bed
brought back to flesh
I hear her message sidle up my spine
and beat upon
the drum that is my skull. I pound
my pillow, pull skin out from my neck
and it does not spring back.
I might shrink and creep inside
to find what I am looking for:
why the ways the cosmos addresses
me cannot be fingered
but only felt, heavy as a book
of prayer that drops from my hand
the moment I pass on to sleep.

MY FRIENDS HAVE HOLES

. . . cut in the tops of their heads
so the cosmos can send in
its love directly and
when they awake
and lean out the window
they are given a lift

They pull themselves back in
with a laugh on their lips
now they've been connected
—no longer
a solitary fluctuation
inside a well-contained machine
that seeks a flash
from planes up there I can't
imagine

They're waiting for me
to shave and make the incisions
with the homemade kit available
from any faith—and I want to
very much indeed yes I do

because my own head each morning
is muddied, needs light
of the sort I can't
generate on my own, an effort
to believe and make conscious

while thinking mostly about bed
and sleeping or other changes
of the mind: caffeine, wine
eight hours of television
or a wind from the ocean
or a metaphor

PRAYER FOR A FRIEND

He bore the mark of the knife
on the back of his head,
an inverted U like the print
of a horseshoe where the surgeon
had entered his brain and removed
a class 4
malignant tumour that had already
taken peripheral vision on the left.
I couldn't help but look
at the shaved patch
with its metal stitches, my eye
drawn there, as a tongue
inserts itself into a cavity.

We talked of past and future,
with words only friends can use
—terminal, tomorrow,
radiation, memory—and I found
my fingers were digging on their own
into the fabric of the blanket
covering the couch: they found holes
in the knotty
knitted material. I needed to dig

and cling, thinking of his wife
in the kitchen, making a pale tea.

My cornea is distorted by the steroids,
he says, and so the house
is full of people; he sees one now
sitting between us, a young boy
from the 50's, clean and strong
as if this is an angel of his
former self come to bring him love,
not just electrical hallucinations,
not mere emanations from his need
to keep his spirit strong.

On the drive home I go through
a red light. No one runs into me.
I hit no one. I pull to the curb, panting
a bit, my hands fighting the wheel.
It comes down to this:
I am lucky. Sometimes it happens that way,
my own angel directing everyone
to tasks that take them elsewhere.
Dear angel, I promise to look out more;
thank you and now, please, I release you
from your charge of me so you may
fly to my friend and touch his head.

CROWS DO NOT HAVE RETIREMENT

"There are no words to capture the infinite depth of
crowiness in the crow's flight."

—*Ted Hughes, Winter Pollen*

Crows do not have retirement
homes to go to when finally
their wings break down

No one takes them in
with a sigh and says
sit here for a bit

while I bring you
a cup of raw worm
to help keep your head

swivelling, on the lookout
for fledglings or the dead,
the eagle making you

flock and dive
that white untouchable pate
No one guides them gently

into their last years,
takes account of their
final movements or hears

their calls, their stout beaks
opening without sound
as if thirsting,

their inky heads against
the starchy white linen,
constant television nearby

They fold up in the curb
in the August heat,
the sheen gone from wings

they no longer lift
out of the heap
no other crow will touch

nor even admit,
passing by without
an exploratory peck

leaving their own kind
to gulls, rats, worms, the municipality
To keep the black

ideal of ravenousness
alive, they hop and lift off
and cruise past windows

where old men catch their flash
and are sent off dreaming
of their own unequalled speed and grace

the guns they once held
in their long arms and the damage
they shook from the air

THE DRAMA

He wants to withdraw from
the drama of existence,
from the pain of those
with bent necks

and those who bend necks
into the fire
He opens his eyes
on the day a friend

dies, and feels the invisible
enter his body
through the heart
which leaps in fear

Thus he receives the letter
from the future and it makes
many small points among
the large:

select a morning
and draw its light around you
so you may never forget
the warmth of the earth

you are leaving, so you can
carry rain in your hands
and the memories of rain
into the closed world

THE ART OF DEATH IN LIFE

Home from the wars of the office
he feels again a rebuff
and thinks further of his own failed
response; such sensitivities require
either a change of character
or a little deadness
so he can't replay
a tossed-off word
that went in and laid him low
and caused him later to brood.

One day of the news
and we'd be dead: the quake in Iran,
killers on the loose, kids
lost or shot up, a moment
going strange. We drown
a little in our coffee
to get past the CBC morning
that spills into the sink
or on the floorboards of a taxi,
on concrete, in the brutal sheds
and camps; whoever continues to live,
raise your hand like a white flag and wiggle
your fingers one two three.

A child dies suddenly or even an aunt
and we haven't time to prepare.
The phone rings and without thinking,
without putting on the proper
layer of protection, we pick up
the ringing thing just to shut
it down, we hold it to our head,
stick it right in our ear and wait
for the report to go bang—
feel a big fleshy hand
push on our head and pluck
at our legs so we sink into a chair,
then pull out drawers
and throw open cupboards
reach deep in closets
past vain clothes and try again
to find that vestment we know
will fit only us. We struggle
into armour and straighten up
and before the metal stiffens and hardens
our resolve, we give one last shudder,
that gift going out to the world
to tell where we are to be found.

TIME OVER EARTH

Above bank after bank of cloud
and the sudden open hole for rock or snow,
his seat partner
wrestles newspaper into a fold,
and in the cockpit the first officer
fights ennui and gazes into the round faces
of his instruments as they cast upon him
their evening glow, their eagerness
to serve. The steward from first class
offers comments from the passengers
on the delicacy of the flight,
the sureness of the surge, the persuasiveness
of their arc in and out of heaven.

Meanwhile in seat 16A
the view slips
into darkness once more,
forcing the eyes back from the vista.
His worries resurface
in this airy world
of alloy and wine, foam seats and hard-eyed
understanding focused in the one-brain
of the crew. A beam, he thinks, will soon
pick them up and lead them down,

and they will stay fastened
to this hope.

They rush to smell the new city—or the same one
returned to, which he re-enters
unchanged by time over earth; he knew
the thin light reaching into black
had not touched him
when he swept through revolving doors
in no less hurry
than other earthling friends.
Now asleep in his bed
his body floats
across space, trying to arrive
on time, not caught
by the trees reaching up
to tear and throw him open.
Motionless under quilt, on pillow,
his eyes repeat all he has seen
and feared to see, each breath
hanging out of his body
in the worst kind of silent air.

THE SON

That night
I came to a white room
and saw upon a couch
shaped like a wave
the son I never had
curled thin as tissue, his eyes
closed. The light
fell from some high
window—just one:
tall, stained, opaque—
so his face shone
yet looked like mine.

His name is Ian
or perhaps Ian David
or Wolfgang—some Teutonic
fellow who came straight
out of me dressed in white
not moving when I reach out
and touch him, my hand
passing through his linen
and his flesh. He looks
content, almost a swain,
but I doubt he's learned much

all those years with his eyes closed.
What he missed of sun and bread
perhaps he dreams, great fields
he can scheme up.
The look on his face tells me
he is alive in there.

                    Is it better
that you feel no cold nor question,
cannot rise off that couch
but stay caught up
in dreams if dreams there are
in your white world? How can you
stay so long in that repose,
arm bent behind your head?

Perhaps after a time
you are redeployed, lifted
away from me, called by
some salty embrace into a country
I will never visit, its white sun
every day entering your eyes
and tugging you naturally
into the affections of the flesh.
Will you sink into a bed and dream
of me, of who you might have been
in other circumstances; you dream

of snow your country rarely sees,
which draws you northward
at an early age, your crayons
making the ground a blue of the early
winter which your friends
make green with grass.

THE OPTIONS

When you die
here are the options:
everything or oblivion

A centre of light and around it
all you love, those dead
and those abiding still
and each holding
an object of endearment
you lost long ago
before you came to
know and be simultaneously
at last
at rest
beyond words

Or else your cells
stop their chemical
talk, the neurons say no
and their warmth leaves you
not with black
not even the absence of black—
nothing of earth's up, round, biomass, span
just the nonexistence

you tried to conjure once
by closing your eyes and
sleeping, except that dreams
fired their figments
across space at you
and your muscles straining

While we live
we pick one of these options
to live by, and neither is understood
the way the robin in the tree is
who speaks to us of March lust,
the way water and clouds are
which tell us to walk out
into the day, how to step
on grass and mud and feel the pull
upward and then sag an hour later
down, we with our little time
and our ideas and our blood